ANOTHER
PLANET EARTH

ANOTHER
PLANET EARTH

NEW AND SELECTED POEMS

DAVID MORPHET

First published in 2018 by

Notion Books
11 Daisy Lane
London
SW6 3DD
www.notionbooks.co.uk

Copyright © David Morphet 2018

The right of David Morphet to be identified as the author of this work
has been asserted by him in accordance with the Copyright, Designs and
Patents Act 1988

All rights reserved. No part of this book may be reproduced, stored in a
retrieval system, or transmitted, in any form or by any means, without the
prior permission in writing of the author. Requests to publish work from
this book should be made to Notion Books.

ISBN 978-0-9575458-5-4

Design by Helen Swansbourne

The Silence of Xylem appeared in *The London Magazine*. *How good he was*
appeared in the *TLS* and *Trust the engineers* in *Ingenia*. *The Silence of Xylem,
No Mangos in Tibet* and *Going Critical* appeared in translation in the
Russian magazine *Noviy Mir*. A number of poems from *A sequence from the
Cyclades* [2012] have been set to music in a song cycle by the composer
Adrian Rickard.

As of mid-2018 there were over 3,500
confirmed planets in over 2,500 systems.
It has been hypothesized that there
are several billions of potentially
habitable Earth-sized planets
in the Milky Way

By the same author:

Poetry
Seventy-Seven Poems
The Angel and the Fox
Approaching Animals from A to Z
39 Ways of Looking
The Silence of Green
The Maze – a daydream in five cantos
The Intruders and other poems
Lyrics from the Periodic Table
A Sequence from the Cyclades
Night Train to Utopia and other tales
Satires and Legacies
Homecoming by Microlight – Landscapes and Satires
Brief Encounters
The Wranglers and other poems

Biography
Louis Jennings MP,
Editor of the *New York Times* and Tory Democrat

Born in Yorkshire, David Morphet read English at Cambridge where he was co-editor of the literary magazine *Delta*. In the early 1960s he occasionally attended meetings of *The Group*, and some years ago was a Board member of *Magma*. He has worked in the British Diplomatic Service, has represented the United Kingdom on various international energy bodies, and has worked in the power and construction industries. He was a founder member and early chairman of a charity concerned with social aspects of severe mental illness. Married, with three grown-up children and five grandchildren, he lives in London.

Some comments on David Morphet's previous collections

Dannie Abse noted *'a great gift for evoking atmosphere'* in ***Seventy-Seven Poems*** and found ***The Silence of Green*** *'a remarkable book, its sequences all of a piece'.*

Fergus Allen found ***The Angel and the Fox*** *'verbally dexterous and intellectually satisfying'.*

Michael Hamburger found ***39 Ways of Looking*** *'magnanimous and intelligent'.*

David Holbrook found ***The Angel and the Fox*** *'full of an irony about experience that demands close attention'.*

Alan Jenkins found ***Night Train to Utopia*** *'impressive, ambitious and elegantly done'.*

Karl Miller found the poems and stories in ***Night Train to Utopia*** *'ingenious and elegant'.*

Michael Symmons Roberts found ***The Maze*** *'a terrific piece of work for its ambition, poise and great formal skill'.*

George Szirtes observed that the ***Lyrics from the Periodic Table*** *'sit at a fascinating angle to the normal concerns of poetry'.*

Charles Tomlinson was *'struck by the quality and distinction of the poetry'* in ***The Silence of Green***.

Anthony Thwaite admired *'the pertinacity of observation and clear lines'* of ***The Silence of Green.***

Daniel Weissbort wrote in a review of ***The Silence of Green*** in *PN Review* that what [Morphet] accomplishes is *of considerable significance, re-directing our attention to what is about us ... He writes with care and above all love and compassion.*

Contents

New Poems

Another Planet Earth: a sequence of twenty poems

Synopsis	16
What makes the world go round	17
Another Planet Earth	19
Wider spaces	20
New frontiers	21
Headline news	22
Fieldwork	23
Listing the wise	24
Archetypes	25
Barbarians	26
Wholesome	27
When the system's down	28
Retribution	29
Painful memories	30
The highest standards of debate	31
No good at poker	32
The state of the nation	33
Truth and duty	34
Not to be ignored	35
Another dream	36
Habitable zones	37

Poems from the Cyclades

Island of Apollo	39
Visiting Homer's tomb	40
Walls on Andros	41
Metaphoric ferries	42
The sea is master	43

Selected Poems

from *Seventy-Seven Poems* [2002]

Moorland	46
Retreat	48
Nightfall at Pedraza	49
Summer in Cadiz	50
For my pregnant 26	51
Ward visit	52
The child is well	54
My father's signature	56

from *The Angel and the Fox* [2003]

The Angel and the Fox	57
Heroes	59
Audit	60
Compromise	61
Here and Now	62
Swallow-holes	64
Heights	66
An exchange of gifts	67
Speaking for myself	68
Repossession	69
Back again	70

from *Approaching animals from A to Z* [2004]

Restlessness	71
Chameleon	73
Geese	74
Honey-bee	75
Inchworm	76
Newt	77
Rat	78
Starlings	79

from *39 Ways of Looking* [2005]

Vincent's chair	81
Shamans	82
Kyoto garden	83
Pen-y-ghent	84
Winter day above Dent	85
Haikus for a summer day	86
Open the atlas	87

from *The Silence of Green* [2007]

Lebensraum	88
The Silence of Xylem	89
It doesn't know when to stop	90
No Mangos in Tibet	91
Welwitschia to Bristlecone	92
Bonsai at Wisley	93
Ages of Oak	94
The ambition of Ivy	95
Ode to the Artichoke	96
An Aloe in Natal	98
Moor song	99
Song of wool	100
Consolations	101
My private island	103
Nuance	104
What they settled for	105
Going critical	106

Extracts from *The Maze – a daydream in five cantos* [2009]

	107

from *The Intruders* [2010]

Just tell them what they want to hear	109
Turning a blind eye	110
How good he was	111
Trust the engineers	112
from *Five Songs for Sarah*	
i. Marmalade	113
ii. Wicken jelly	114
Return to the Pennines	115

from *Lyrics from the Periodic Table* [2011]

A song for oxygen	116
The inertia of argon	117
Stardust calcium	118
The charms of zinc	119
Adieu to mercury	120

from *A sequence from the Cyclades* [2012]

Islands rise at dawn	121
High wind on Serifos	122
Possession	123
Dusk in Naxos	124
Winds on Naxos	125
A ring of islands	126

Extract from *Night Train to Utopia and other tales* [2013]   127

from *Satires and Legacies* [2014]

Extract from *Purdue's Tale*	129
A Master Chef with grand designs	131
There was a state that lost its head	133
Inheritance; and A few words of praise	134
From *Exchanges with Angel*	
So late in life	135
A warning	136
Full and final settlement	137

from *Homecoming by Microlight* [2015]

Resurrection at Dent	138
Extract from *Steel-capped PR*	139
Out of sight	141

from *Brief Encounters* [2016]

Willy Brandt comes for breakfast 1967	142
Greeting Monty 1967	144
On not meeting Ronald Reagan 1991	145

from *The Wranglers* [2017]

7.	Corruption	146
11.	*A hundred things to do before you die*	147
17.	He just won't stop	149
18.	*Lighten up!*	150
20.	Impatient capital	151
25.	Grievance	153
28.	Will you fight?	154
29.	Catching the tide	156
30.	Vision	157
	Contracted out	158
	Ode to the higher gardening	160

Preface

New Poems

A sequence of twenty poems extends the sharp debate between the aspiration of Angel and the skulduggery of Fox which began with *The Angel and the Fox* [2003] and is a leading feature of *The Intruders* [2010] and *The Wranglers* [2017]. Angel, impassioned by the need for *'vision and discovery'*, is excited by the chances of finding and learning from *'another Planet Earth'* in a *'habitable zone'* of some distant star. But his enthusiasm wanes as he comes to recognise the risks *'here and now'* to our own *'safely-habitable zones'* and changes course. From now on he plans to look for ways to *'calibrate and scale/ terrestrial malfunction'*.

The five poems which follow were inspired by a recent visit to the Greek Cyclades and complement *A sequence from the Cyclades* [2012].

Selected Poems

The ninety or so poems selected from my previous fourteen collections highlight themes which over the years have worked strongly on my imagination. Some of the earlier Angel and Fox poems are here with their contrast of ambitious endeavour with trickery. Other leading themes are the vital importance of the 'green silence' of the world of plants in circumscribing the cacophony of modern life, the restlessness of the animal kingdom, the immense power of the one hundred or so elements listed in the Periodic Table, and the deep influence of landscape on mood and thought.

There are also a number of personal poems and a certain amount of satire. The longer satirical and other narratives in *The Maze* [2009], *Night Train to Utopia* [2013], *Satires and Legacies* [2014] and *Homecoming by Microlight* [2015] do not lend themselves easily to abbreviation but short extracts have been included from a number of the narratives.

A note on composition

I aim for plain modern diction. Rhyme features strongly, whether end-rhyme or slant-rhyme or internal thyme, and everywhere I have an ear to assonance. I find my poems often fall easily into quatrains and tercets and on occasion I follow strict forms such as *terza rima* (throughout *The Maze*) and villanelle (eg *How good he was!*). Much of my later work is not lyrical. Not that I have ceased to be attracted by the inwardness of the lyrical but my interests have moved increasingly towards observation of human behaviour from a certain distance – what I think of as 'a position of witness'.

I extend warm thanks to all who have commented helpfully on my work and particularly to Bryan Hopkinson and Michael Shaw. I also acknowledge wise counsel in years gone by from the late Michael Baldwin and the late Dan Jacobson.

New Poems

Another Planet Earth:
a sequence of twenty poems

Synopsis

The first poem in the sequence echoes the last poem in the sequence in *The Wranglers* [2017] where Angel is seen to be impassioned by the need for '*vision and discovery*'.

The theme of discovery leads to three poems on Angel's excitement about the chances of finding and learning from '*another Planet Earth*' in the '*habitable zone*' of some distant star.

Eight poems follow on his curiosity about areas such as anthropology, psychology, and literary deconstruction.

The thirteenth poem, recording Angel's regret at things he has said and done in the past, leads to three poems on his discontent with the nation's affairs.

Atmosphere shifts in the final four poems. A strong expression of Angel's faith in truth and duty is followed by two unsettling dreams. The final poem shows his enthusiasm for '*another Planet Earth*' waning as he comes to recognise the risks to our own '*safely-habitable zones*'. He changes course and plans in future to look for ways to '*calibrate and scale/ terrestrial malfunction*'.

Fox, who provides cynical counterpoint throughout, laughs at this. Angel retorts that

'*Confidence is wearing thin/ on prospects for a stable Earth./ And we have no other.*'

What makes the world go round

Fox and Angel come round unannounced
as if they own the place.
I can't help listening.

Angel's constant theme is joy of spirit –
the delight that visionaries feel
when new paths open for the mind.

He claims what makes the world go round
is *vision's metaphysical excursions*
and quiverings at what may come to be.

Impatient for a strong pulse of discovery
he dotes on astrophysical research
and Hubble's glorious images. He talks
incessantly of *parsecs* and *albedo*
and holds it won't be long before
another Planet Earth's revealed
among the exoplanet swarms,
yielding *amazing answers*
to terrestrial **hows** and **whys**.

And constantly his thoughts revolve
round ways of mending governance
and wholesale self-improvement.

Not so with Fox whose thoughts revolve
round crooked covert offshore deals
with funds unmodified by tax,
massaged through numbered bank accounts
of phantom corporations.
His vision is of *fabulous returns.*

It/

It irks him to hear Angel advocate
abstractions such as social equity.
That's all hot air he tells himself.
What really makes the world go round
is graft and bluster and deceit and greed.
The proof is everywhere.

Another Planet Earth

Nothing would please Angel more
than news a planet has been found
with oceans lapping sandy shores.
He scans all scientific prints
for word of objects circling stars
with habitable atmospheres.
He calls these *signals from the front*
and holds that astrophysicists
will one day net another Earth.

Suppose they do says Fox. *So what?*
The cosmos may have Earths galore
we'll find at astronomic cost
but none with any sign of life –
none of them worth waiting for.

But Angel thinks that *searching stirs*
the philosophic mind.
We have a deep-felt need to know
if we're alone or one of multitudes.
And what those multitudes may be.
The answer may be very close.

It won't be anything like clear
jeers Fox.

Wider spaces

Discovery-addicted Angel cites
Drake's dogged, dog-leg circumnavigation,
Cook hitting on Australia's missing hem,
and spacecraft skirting rings and moons of Saturn.
These epics, he pronounces, *drive our minds*
from looking inward, into wider spaces.
And the urge to seek and find is nothing new.
Think of the star-charts of Chaldean sages.

Fox laughs. *Behind that drive lies greed*
for power – empire – and control.
Chaldean calculators took their cue
from priests and priestly ritual.
Behind space rockets you will find
a stellar cloud of generals.

That's less than half the story Angel cries.
Discovery's the axis around which
the whole of human life revolves.
We enter new worlds with delight.

And a blind eye to Pandora's Box says Fox.
Discovery may prove to be
at bottom wholly mischievous.
And no way can you put it back.

New frontiers

Gazing at the night sky, Angel scans
the zodiac from Capricorn to Gemini.
Impassioned by astronomy he charts
the fire of suns and blaze of galaxies.
There simply is no thrill he tells himself
like viewing from a ringside seat
the circus of creation.
Avidly he seizes on all news
of exoplanet shape and size.
That is where he tells himself,
we'll soon be crossing new frontiers.

Fox finds him wide-eyed with a catalogue
of telescopes and jeers
What's the point of watching stars
that simply fire up, blaze and disappear?
Leave space stuff to the specialists!
*What **matters** is to stop large rocks*
from pulverising Earth.
*You can't do **that!***

Headline news

Angel craves discovery. He notes
It's never less than headline news
when the skull turns up of some new hominid.

Nowhere can you find a better tale
than evolution to enthuse the mind.
Just think of the shapes encased in fossil shales
and all the evidence that's come to light
of the fits and starts of natural selection.

Fox listens but soon loses interest.

All that chasing after ancient bones he sneers
tells nothing of what's coming next.
It's a guidebook for survival that we need –
on how to cope with global ash or flood
or nuclear winter or a rock from space.
Odds on we'll end up like the dinosaurs
and make our own distinctive contribution
to the fossil catalogue.

Fieldwork

Scanning Malinowski's seminal
Sexual Life of Savages in New Guinea,
Angel's chastened that he knows so little.
He sends for Mead's book on Samoa
and makes a start on *The Golden Bough*.
He skims through *Totem and Taboo*.
He reads the works of Levi-Strauss.
Burning midnight oil, he studies
complicated laws of kin,
rites of passage, rites of death,
drawn from fieldwork in Dahomey
and studies of the Cree and Iroquois.
Humans he concludes *are all the same*
except – he pauses – *where they're clearly not.*

Fieldwork? sniggers Fox. *I'll tell you this.*
I've closely watched the local tribes for years.
Some have habits that are quite appalling
and there's not a single one of them I'd trust.

Listing the wise

Angel's drawing up a list of those
reputed to be wise, and why.
It's odd how few there are he notes
who really qualify.
(He rates a threat to chop a child in half
exceptionally primitive.)
And so-called *sayings of the wise* seem trite
and all too often trotted out
in fortune cookies or on greeting cards.

He's coming to believe the really wise
are those who say they're only on the edge
of knowing anything at all.

*It's **thinking** of a list* he tells himself
that matters. Not completing it.

Fox has his own idea of those
deserving to be rated really smart.
Monopolists who squeeze their captive markets.
Lawyers who find ways to slip past tax.

Archetypes

Today sees Angel deep in Jung.
He's grown enthused by dream analysis
and checks on all the archetypes,
sensing a kind of personal rapport
with the image of the Wise Old Man.
He muses on the Anima and Shadow
and meanings of the Mandala.
He'd like to take a lengthy dip
into deep seas of the Unconscious
and rise up glorious on a Venus shell
of shining, oceanic truth.

Fox spies his far-off look and asks
if he has seen a ghost – or what?
Angel stares and suddenly exclaims
Your aura is an image of the Trickster –
Loki, an eternal archetype!
You're a classic subject for the couch.
You ought to see a psychoanalyst.

Fox hasn't understood a word.
Not me he says. *I never get depressed.*

Barbarians

Angel's troubled by Cavafy's tale
of a city in paralysis
awaiting onslaught by barbarians.
Yet when the wild men fail to come
its people are directionless and moan
What now is to become of us?
At least the wild men were a kind of answer.

Angel finds the tale *contemptible.*
Barbarians offer no kind of solution
to state inertia or to anything.
Solutions lie in public works like drains
and unremitting civic education.

That's hopelessly conventional! snarls Fox.
From time to time you need to shake things up
or else the patterns never change.
And change means opportunities
to those with wits to seize them.
Barbarians? So what? Just bring them on!

Wholesome

Angel's wary about words like *wholesome*
which might well be in common use
by lyrical nutritionists
or in discourse between prudish monsignori
but won't be found in works of deconstruction.

He's learning to watch language carefully
reading between the lines for intertext.

He hums a little to compose his thoughts.
Then counts off on his fingers one by one ...

B for Barthes and D for Derrida.
He hesitates on E but settles for
Ecole Normale Supérieure.
Then F (Foucault) and K (Kristeva) but
he doubts he'll ever come to be
a deconstruction groupie.

Now *wholesome's* not an adjective for which
Fox has ever sought or found a purpose.
He likes a dubious edge to things
and words that smell of profit.

When the system's down

Computer-challenged Angel groans.
He says he'd like a robot standing by
to help him when the system's down.

Be careful what you wish for mutters Fox.
It won't be long before A.I. outstrips
the circuits of the human brain.
You may find you're outwitted
by your electronic friend.

Angel listens hard and changes gear.
But how on earth he asks
*could **that** occur?*
*For **that** a robot surely needs to be –*
he hesitates – ***aware****.*

Fox, who keeps abreast of things, responds
Through unremitting simulation
robots will come to mimic all we do.
And this he adds *will not be cause*
for human celebration.

Angel finds for once he's lost for words.

Retribution

Angel's hard-line about retribution.
He urges *condign punishment* for crime.
An eye for an eye is no bad way, he thinks,
to deal with hardened criminals.
We need a system that is cut and dried
and doesn't yield to misplaced sentiment.

And though he wobbles every time
he comes to hear of mitigating facts
which justify *occasional exceptions,*
he won't let *minor detail* overturn
his settled bearings and convictions.
The wicked have to suffer he declares.
How else can you induce them to repent?

Repentance has no place in Fox's book
nor does he give unnecessary thought
to pros and cons of penal retribution.
For him the most important thing
is making doubly sure you don't get caught.

But ask about revenge – you'll find that Fox
is ready to discuss all ways and means
of what he views as *necessary business.*

Painful memories

For all his virtue, Angel knows
at times he's been incautious and erratic.
He shudders as he thinks how close he's come
to pitfall and discredit
and hankers deeply after a better past –
a general clean-up of his personal file
with memory deletions dating back
to the dawn of indiscretion.

Fox spots him brooding. He's intrigued.
Why such a funeral face? he asks.
Is something lost or missing?
Not what you'd think says Angel with a glare.
I'm going over painful memories
of words I let slip that I now regret.
But no – no object's lost.
That's not the sting.

I too have painful memories says Fox
of fouled-up schemes and deals that failed.
But looking back and brooding? Not a chance.
Better to make sure at the next chicane
some other punter tumbles.

The highest standards of debate

Angel takes to writing memoranda
on news he picks up in the local press
on planning applications and inquiries.
He posts these off in various directions
to *people who he's sure will want to read*
entirely public-spirited advice
from one who seeks to make a contribution
to the highest standards of debate.
He's passionate about the force of reason.
A well-framed argument he holds
can scarcely fail to carry weight.

But it seems that all his careful work –
his keen analysis – his telling points –
if read at all – is having no effect.

Fox says he knows how arguments are won
and who'll be on the winning side.
It's down he claims *to debts called in.*
It's down to favours that are owed.
The people who'll decide expect to find
the answers in brown envelopes.
Well-framed analysis? Key points? Dream on!

No good at poker

Irritably, Angel scans
the news for the latest sleight-of-hand,
smoke-and-mirror schemes and spin
from Ministers and Government.

It's all deceit! (His face grows puce –
his words turn blue.) *And getting worse!*
Fox warns him *Simmer down friend, or
you'll end up in intensive care.*

*It's not my nature to stay calm –
I need to make my feelings plain*
says Angel *when I see what tricks
are played, and what's at stake.*

*Undoubtedly you have the right
to criticise and speak your mind
and show exactly how you feel –
but you'd be no good at poker* murmurs Fox.

The state of the nation

Make no mistake! dyspeptic Angel growls.
We're tied in ever-tightening knots.
We're in the grip of counterfeit.
We've let ourselves be taken in
by chancers, cheats and parasites.
We've fallen for the sly deceits
of fabulists and loud-mouthed fools.
The nation's growing stiff with debt
and the blood of self-inflicted wounds.

Hold on! cries Fox. *There is no call*
for such ill-tempered spluttering!
Ridding the state of bloat and fat
is not a self-inflicted wound.
It's down to private enterprise to drive
the pistons of tomorrow's growth,
incentivised by public debt.
Financing burdens can be left he adds
for later times to liquidate.

I see! snaps Angel. *Leave our kids to pay!*
They're going to find that hard to take.
I see no sign of any silver lining.
It won't be long before the howls. Just wait!

Truth and duty

Angel has a vast regard for truth
and idealises duty.
These, he holds, are *the things by which we live*.

He sees truth as an anchorage
and duty as a magnetic force
that draws stray impulse-filings into place.
Together they deliver *what is right*.

He looks for ballast to philosophy.
Just now he's muttered *Plato*, *Kant*,
Imperative and *Categorical*.

Fox leers. His view of truth is flexible.
He's all in favour where it has a market value.
In which case he asserts it should come out
in small instalments sensitively priced.

His view of duty's purposefully vague
but for Angel he's begun to feel
a modicum of guarded admiration.
I've come to think he says *from time to time
a man who's known to keep his word
could prove distinctly useful*.

Not to be ignored

Angel's bewildered by the eulogy.
It's not of anyone he knows but here he sits
tight-packed in the principal mourners' row
of a chapel of remembrance.
The names he hears are unfamiliar.
He's lost his glasses and can't read the hymns.
Yet worse. Heads turn to him and nod
as if he occupied some special place
in the life of the deceased.
He's sitting tight. It's the only way to cope.
He knows he'll shortly have to stand in line
as all express condolences.

Later he tells Fox of his troubling dream.
It's most unusual he says *to find myself
in situations I don't understand
and circumstances which I can't control.*

Fox, superstitious, holds his tongue.
Dreams of death are deep is what he thinks,
and not to be ignored.

Another dream

Angel has a second warning dream.
It shakes him to the core.
He finds that he's alone on stage
confronting an expectant audience
and no idea of what he's meant to say.
The lights are dimmed down in the hall
and turned up on his chair.
He's paralysed.

He can't remember how the nightmare ends
but takes it as a sign he's far too slow
to deal with pitfall and surprise –
too ill-prepared and unspontaneous.
I need he says *to be more purposeful.*
I need a programme of reform.

Fox doesn't like the sound of things
like programmes of reform.
He'd much prefer the Angel stay
with joy of vision and his head in stars.
You're reading far too much into
a gurgling in the pipes he says.
Dreams are a dumping-ground
for every kind of garbage.
Let it go!

Habitable zones

Angel, jolted, says he's moving on.
He needs to find *some quiet place*
away from mesmerising spin
where he can *bit by bit* collect his thoughts
and *bring them home.*

That won't be moving on says Fox.
You'll find you're rambling round a track
of endless introspection.
He urges Angel to relax –
You really need to throttle back!
Be easy on yourself!
I'll show you how!
Just give up all those useless games with words
which never lead to anything.

Your ways says Angel *are not mine.*
It's purpose that I'm seeking, not evasion.
A new account of things. A new direction.

I think laughs Fox *you're dreaming of*
another Planet Earth that wouldn't
give us grief like this one!

It's true says Angel *that I sometimes dream*
of how another Earth might look
and how in time discovery may yield
formidable conclusions.

And no doubt exoplanets will be found
which stir us to the core though none may show us
mirrors without flaws or offer
cause for celebration.

Meanwhile/

Meanwhile not light-years off but here and now
our fractured planet lacks control
and certainty we can sustain
safely-habitable zones.

Fox laughs again and jeers *I see!*
There is no wonderful new Earth!
It seems your wisdom's wearing thin!

Not so says Angel. *It's been re-assigned.*
My vision now is fully trained
on ways to calibrate and scale
terrestrial malfunction.

Fox says he can't believe his ears.
*You won't get far with **that*** he laughs.

Perhaps says Angel *But the stage is set.*
Confidence is wearing thin
on prospects for a stable Earth.
And we have no other.

Poems from the Cyclades

Island of Apollo

It's May on Delos and the island air
is carrying faint scents of spring
from meagre vegetation.
Lizards scuttle into banks of thorn.

Eager Hellenists stride out
past ruined temples, tumbled walls,
down paths of scattered stone and myth,
stirred by the Homeric hymn
to Delian Apollo.
Boat after boat from Mykonos
bring them to this landing-place
of long imagination.

Here was the Cycladean heart.
For silvered centuries it pulsed
with cult and trade and slavery
till pirates tore the place apart,
leaving broken stone and shard
in the hands of archaeologists.
Oh! how scholars would rejoice
should careful trowelling turn up
some fragment of Euripides
or a *paean* to Apollo!

Visiting Homer's tomb

Herodotus perhaps was taken in
when they told him *Homer's sacred head*
was laid here in this ragged tomb.
Some claim there was no *sacred head* at all,
that Homer is a literary myth,
a sort of bardic composite.
If so, it's whimsical to visit here.

But well up with the view from Sounion,
across the far horizon sail
flagships of the Cyclades.
Hulls of Poros and of Naxos rise
lined up in long flotilla.
And down there in the open sea
imagination conjures up
Odysseus' cockleshell.

Homer's sacred head or not,
this headland is a place where time
may, an instant, hold its breath.

Walls on Andros

Where sea allows, there's level sand.
Elsewhere, throughout the island, rock –
colossal boulders, turrets , crags,
smooth-bodied outcrops humped like whales,
scattered rubble, heaped debris,
scree tumbling down in smithereens.
Between the contours, little grass.
The only certain crop is stone.

Piling sharp-edged slab on slab
Andriots have given shape
to chaos with long lines of wall,
threading it with paths of slate.
But there's no end of rock. Enough remains
to build a whole metropolis.

Metaphoric ferries

Island ferries are no more
than metaphor for brisk exchange.
Day by day huge trucks reverse
slowly up through ferry jaws
into the hollow gut within.

Entirely functional
these sea-pantechnicons.
Prosaic and routine the way
they throb and churn
the quayside waters.

There's no romance in their discharge of trucks
and spew of jostling passengers.
Dreams of sailing into Delos
with a cargo of apes and ivory
can be put on hold.

The sea is master

Time and again
throughout unquiet centuries
the islands have changed hands
as empires have come and gone.
But the sea was always master.

Hidden claws of rock defend
their shores against aggression.
The wrecks they've claimed are numberless.
Waters of the Cyclades
are strewn with skeletons.

Today the islands like to think
they're self-contained
and manage very well if left alone.
But to the sea they stay subservient.
It's always master.

Selected Poems

from *Seventy-Seven Poems* [2002]

Moorland

The moor has a dialect
abrupt and guttural,
harsh and impoverished.

It is the sharp tongue of the wind
berating the bracken
and the yatter of rain.

It is the hawk's cry,
and the hare's scream,
and the low cough of grouse.

Swarthy the moor's complexion,
its skin of peat
pocked with reed colonies,

and heather primed
for autumn's explosion
into purple erysipelas.

It partners the sky.
The two of them cohabit,
blend and intersect.

The morning mist
brings a confinement
of all horizons;

while the wester sun
burns its image
on the moorland pools.

This unhedged margin
is our borderland
and needful wilderness.

May its rough thirst
never be slaked by fertile lime,
or by the dew of pasture.

Retreat

Squat and silent, Celtic farms
keep their own counsel;
stand on the hill's flank
like sentinels.

No Saxon clusters,
village green.
Here, the single hearth
and song unseen.

Silence and isolation;
life is close and thick
as the slow smoke
rising from their stacks.

Planetary farms
skirting the dark moors,
take me aboard, close me
within your habitable silence.

Nightfall at Pedraza

The sun's disc drops
behind the curtain of the hills;
wild thyme and lavender grow strong.
In the village square and alleyways
Children are called in from their games.

Soon we are head up in a bowl of stars.
We cannot hear the streams below
but know along which moonlit roads they lie.
The headlamps of a distant car
sway like a drunken meteor.

Across the fields the graveyard stands
square in the shadow of its walls.
Widows who pay court daily to the dead
are now back through the postern gate.
There is no wind: a prayer would last the night.

That is the only bitter land around.
Thank God we are still alive to hear
the dry pulse of the earth.
And while we listen, and the moon
tilts her dish of light

on the hills, and the sweet herbs
mingle in still air,
let us hope and love
and take our fill
of what is now and sure

Summer in Cadiz

Cadiz, with its sweet salt breeze,
pecking like a gull at the ocean's edge.
The town is always looking out,
framed by the wide bay and the sea,
instead of Spain's still fields
with their closed horizons.

As if a great door opens,
the Atlantic breeze
is sweeping through its streets
with a cool draught of relief.
I hold the sun in a golden glass
and honour all things maritime.

For my pregnant 26

Briskly kicking you,
this moving fruit,
bonded with water
in your belly's husk,
growing between us
draws us both together.
The words I know for you
have richly multiplied,
born of this child
and your helpless pride in it.
Your ripeness plucks
my swelling love:
the branches of my blood
are heavy with it.

Ward visit

Entering, we leave behind
the familiar ground
of easy conversation.

Here are no well-defined
rules for calling round
on a social occasion.

The room is lined with chairs,
each one apart, as if
in mutual dislike.

By some we're met with stares,
others are still and stiff;
but all of them alike

incurious and sedated.
We find a private space
for our quiet meeting

where little can be stated
beyond the shallow grace
of a simple greeting.

Slowly we navigate
the silences and tour
blind alley and dead end,

seeking words to ungate
response; words to unmoor
affection; words that can mend.

Each visit is a quest,
a pilgrimage to find
in unpromising land

the relics which attest
to a coherent mind
and power to understand.

The child is well

As morning breaks, the nightmare sign;
the arching of the baby's spine;

the blue-tinged lips; the pallid face;
the chill of fear; the rush and race.

The silence in the hospital.
The nurse alert, the doctor still.

The lumbar tap; disease is strong;
the child is weak; the odds are long.

There is no antidote to quell
the virus's invasive swell.

The X-ray, penicillin; tube;
and sterile incubator cube.

The pathos of an infant placed
in isolation and encased.

The crisis at its height. His form
convulsing in the viral storm.

The vigil throughout night and day
before the small shape, screened away.

The hands unable to caress
the infant in his loneliness.

As long hours pass, the growth of hope
strengthened by love, its isotope.

The lungs will fill; the heart will beat;
tomorrow shall bring death's retreat.

The storm subsides; the air grows calm.
The infant stretches, free from harm.

Kind hands now lift him from his cell.
We thank the Lord: the child is well.

My father's signature

The hand is steady
with each letter formed
in the mould of fifty years.
'A' starts off surely on its way:
the 'M' and 'o' curl confidently round;
stutter through 'r' into the dip of 'p'
and end up calmly 'h','e', 't'.

It shows no mutability.
I know what lies, for all that,
behind the hand's clarity.
Each day he would have looked
at such frail proof of identity
with mortal dismay,
waiting for death's eviction.

His life ran slow,
its end I did not see –
saw only his body and his signature.

from *The Angel and the Fox* [2003]

The Angel and the Fox

My counsellors are the angel and the fox,
the constant listeners-in and whisperers.
At all times they are there, always alert.
They like to do things quietly – a word
in the ear – choose not to be overheard.

Faced with the trap of choice, I listen hard,
first to the one and then the other voice.
Neither is dominant; and each in turn
is plausible. The one has tongues of fire;
the other's down to earth and looks no higher.

The angel's fierce and zealous, makes demands,
plays on the keys of conscience and repute,
knows well the haste and restiveness of skill,
the urge for place, compulsion to outclass,
the will to win, the passion to surpass.

The fox is realist; goes step by step.
He worries at the bones of how, not why;
sucks at the marrow of possibilities.
He knows for certain where the knife cuts best.
He's in no doubt of where the blame will rest.

The angel will not swerve or temporize.
His words are adamant, implacable.
He preaches absolutes and certainties;
states what is right and what is meant to be;
and how without pain there is no ecstasy.

The/

The fox advises what is convenient,
what is the smartest and the quickest fix;
how to attract the eye, and woo the ear;
or, if a point or trick cannot be won,
how to get out, cut losses, and move on.

Unlike the fox, who knows the price of things,
the angel never counts the cost. His vice
is always to rush in with sword and flame.
The fox says, "Watch your step, and go to cover
while the hunt is up – wait till the storm blows over."

The angel urges that the hours are few
and must be filled up to the brow and brim
with labour of mind and heart. The fox's
counsel is to take good time and rest,
husbanding wind and limb for when I'm pressed.

Fox points out pitfalls, pilots through chicanes,
tells me to keep my feet on mother earth.
The angel presses me to take the risks
of depth and altitude, where I shall find
worlds unrevealed to those who lag behind.

Each step I take involves a sharp debate
between the angel and the fox. Nor are
the saints immune. They also have to choose
between first one, and then another, voice
which tries to tell them that they have no choice.

Heroes

Be serious says the angel. *Let me know
your heroes and the reason.*

He sees me being slow,
since heroes are out of season,
and I end up saying so.

No says the angel. *Don't prevaricate,
or try me on with some semantic trick,
hoping I won't decypher it.*

All right I say. *You know who heroes are –
those who put others first, and sometimes die for it.*

Slowly the angel nods, and disappears.
This is the kind of thing he likes to hear.

Audit

The angel's back again, unheralded.
He knocks me up at an ungodly hour
to audit my accounts,
running his lightning fingers down the sheet,
and pointing out some gross deficiencies.

He clicks his tongue at my abysmal
failure to make the assets sweat; derides
my upside-down return on capital,
and points out numerous instances
of blatant double-counting.

A missionary planner, he proclaims
that much, much more is called for – enterprise,
determination, raising my sights and game,
due diligence, and what's long overdue, he says –
fresh vision, with the force to take it through.

Defunct commissions must be written off;
weak lines and unperforming holdings dumped.
Then, with millennial targets set, he disappears
in a cloud of afflatus and elation,
leaving me agitated and depressed.

Compromise

Slowly, and none too fine,
the snail of compromise
has drawn a faint white line
between the noes and ayes.

With sharp bark and soft hiss
of disbelief, the fox
and angel take amiss
a motion that unblocks.

Their nature is to baulk
at middle ways; to see
in terms of cheese and chalk;
to jar and disagree.

This they say is the strength
of politics; to maul
the arguments at length,
and fight it out; winner takes all.

Less ardent spirits burn
more slowly; meet half-way;
and do their best to turn
the cutting edge away.

Here and Now

I stretch out under an oleander's fronds
and yawn with satisfaction, seeing
the blue daub of the bay with its smudge of yachts,
and hearing the café's comfortable sounds.

Backward and forward goes the white-shirted waiter,
ferrying orders round the square.
Here is a fountain, here are pigeons, here a mulberry.
What can I tell of them?

Listening, listening, listening, listening
splutters the fountain as it soars and topples over,
head cocked to one side; immaculate;
never changing, never exactly the same.

It is the admiral of this peaceful shore establishment,
columned and glittering with braid from top to tail;
superbly cool;
and, through the long hours, always keeping watch.

Look at it all, look at it all!
gabble the shifty pigeons, opportunistic,
unstoppably garrulous, strutting, bustling,
eyeing all things with bleak intensity.

They have no past and no tomorrow –
only the next scheme and the next after that.
Houdini with cars, they quickly flutter back
into the ring, and resume their patter.

As for the mulberry, it has no voice,
but drops its soft grenades on the platía
for the sun to fix and blacken, etching
indelible stains. An armadillo

of shade, its leaves reach out and overlap,
trapping the flakes of sunlight in its scales –
only a fragment reaches the mottled stray
sprawled slackly on the pavement, fast asleep.

And how to keep this picture in its frame –
to freeze and file away for greyer days?
Nothing can quite capture it – paint nor pen.
All of our idylls are recalcitrant –

they jib and malinger – won't come when they're called.
And no good trying to turn back the clock –
we're always restless, always moving on.
All changes – men, and mood, and politics.

Pneumatic drills may shatter the fountain,
pierce the mulberry; age may afflict the eye
or the mind's brightness; everything may slip
into a new mode, wiping memory clean.

So, you hospitable oleander –
pink and capacious, richly canopied –
help me to hold this moment as it passes,
hold and intensify the here and now.

Swallow-holes

Our maps define the limestone dale we're in,
and also show us what's beneath the skin
of field and fell. Among the contour lines
are pockmark swallow-holes, like ancient mines.

These are the avens plunging to deep veins
in the rock's fracture; splintered souterrains
spreading across an obscure hinterland.
Unseen, dark rivers flow there; lakes expand.

A world apart, the bowelled aquifers;
the dripping caverns with their long fingers
of lime; the buried waters trickling by
without disturbance; no observing eye

to detect them in their slow processes –
contaminate – pierce their unconsciousness.
Deep below ground, the hidden measures serve
to hold, accumulate, keep in reserve.

And yet the upper landscape answers
to their capacities; the river dries or dances
according to their appetite; it swells
when they are swollen; and when they thirst, it fails.

Explorers I salute; those who descend
and penetrate, and push on to the end,
exhausted, always hoping that beyond a
last dark channel they will find a wonder.

The wonder, though, remains in what's unseen;
the narrow capillaries; the whole machine
with its elaborate vessels, filters
of mineral, rich with minute particulars.

The wonder lies in courses of a deep
and hidden purity, the constant seep
of waters, and in due time their issuing
into a flight of streams, a sudden spring.

Heights

The snow lingers on Lochnagar
though it is spring, and the grouse calls
to its mate. We have risen far
up the mountainside, and I recall

the two of us scaling our first heights,
unready yet to recognise that those
narrow paths of the Dolomites
would lead to our lives' synthesis.

How long ago, those newly-tried
and indeterminate wanderings!
Here you are sure, and by my side
until the final sundering.

You are so much a part of me,
I know that where you stand, I stand.
You are the lens through which I see
love focused till I understand

its sharpness and integrity.
You are my head and heart and hand.
As the snow melts, the stream flows free.
As the hills near, the skies expand.

An exchange of gifts

Our Christmas visit to the nunnery.
In the bare parlour, on their wooden chairs,
bored with unseasonal austerity,
the children fidget, give resentful stares.

Footsteps behind the shuttered double grill.
A question asked, and then the boards fold back,
and tiny, beaming rosy-cheeked Estelle
is there to greet us, wimpled, robed in black.

On our side of the barrier, we bring
tidings of births, engagements, marriages,
and all the canticles of families:
these are the songs she wants to hear us sing.

Her own short antiphon is quickly said:
garden, and holy texts, and holy bread.
Here she has lived for over forty years,
worshipping God and praying for the dead.

The gift we bring her is the tenderness
of children, whom she sees but cannot hold.
The gift she makes to us is innocence,
which we can neither parcel nor enfold.

Speaking for myself

So many years a representative,
speaking in measured tones at many tables;
(I have received instructions to explore ...:
I'm authorised to state that we are able ...)
I think of all the Boards and Councils where,
over those years, I've asked to take the floor,
punctilious in the speeches which I gave,
each nuance shaded, and each caveat clear;

knowing how words can snag on real events,
material outcomes, action in the raw;
shaping a language which would clarify
and not confuse; and should there be a flaw
in the argument, polishing lines-to-take –
the saving mantras which avoid a lie
although they do not fully represent
the fact, and shelter in the formulaic.

Now that I speak for no-one but myself,
I'm still determined to make words obey
the call to focus on elusive thought,
and toe the line on what I want to say.
Suspicious of the imprecise, I seek
to find tools sharp enough to carve what ought
to be given shape; and make them serve
to capture both the literal, and dream, alike.

Repossession

For all these years the silent house has been waiting
                    for its owner to return,
to slide the key in the lock, and raise the long-drawn blinds.

Years have gone slowly by with no sign of domicile.
For years, no one has knocked; for years, no one has spoken.

And now I come into my own, and take possession.
The key turns easily in the lock; the blinds roll back, obedient.

The house has weathered, but is staunch and resilient.
Its furnishings are scant and plain, but serviceable.

The pent-up daylight bursts through every pane.
Reflections, out of check, bolt everywhere.

Arid, in every room, dust begs to be quenched.
Unturned, the quiet taps ache to respond.

Now that I've repossessed the darkened rooms,
no door shall ever be locked; no blind drawn down.

Back again

Just five years after Suez, twenty-one;
night-train to Venice and then sailing on
past the long island flotilla down to Greece;
sidling into Piraeus through the deep canal,
stars bright over the Saronic Gulf;
dining in white tuxedoes.

Here on the waterfront, a limousine
to sweep us to the Parthenon.

Our liner leaves tonight for the Levant.

Now after forty years I'm back again,
this time with boots and haversack,
climbing the narrow streets to the Acropolis,
baklavá spooned from sticky paper bag.

And afterwards by metro to the port,
standing room only.

from *Approaching animals from A to Z* [2004]

Restlessness

All of that kingdom with its straggling phyla,
wandering cohorts and uncouth battalions
defies direction, seethes with restlessness –
hungering, trekking, foraging, migrating.
The only law is one of impetus.
Most of the time it's *sauve qui peut*.

Alluring, though, the swift pulse in muscle,
the ripple and quiver, the flight and attack,
the trembling of wing and cilia,
frenzy of shark and scurry of rat;
the lunge of leopard to the kill;
the feeding python's lengthy peristalsis.

They're like a magnet, all those images
of the anarchic hinterland – the jaws
and fangs and mandibles which microscope
and tele-lens slide under your nose,
drawing you into strange complicity
with carnage. Would you stop it if you could?

Those who see foxes at their serious business
or watch as cats play with the living mouse
approach those wild masks with circumspection
knowing that Eden's nowhere to be found
in that direction. If there is innocence
it's in the viewer's eye, not on the ground.

But/

But still the magnet draws us on.
Hostile, peaceable or parasite,
the restlessness of animals fires up
the pulse of life within us. We respond
with agitation or delight,
charged with their fever and vitality.

Chameleon

Peculiar, the scaly turret eyes
of the chameleon, swivelling
backwards and forwards independently,
projecting into his lizard brain

two sets of images. Yet in attack
he's got the right coordinates to guide
the range and compass of his tight-coiled tongue –
he picks his prey off with a single lunge.

And I too have a variable eye
which looks – looks round – looks past – looks through,
according to my mood and appetite.
At times it verges on reptilian –

predatory, training sight on
the main chance, or given to hard stares
at what is contrary and alien,
or seems to call for a snap judgment.

Geese

Geese – how imperious!
They stretch their necks up high and flap their wings
and hiss and honk and sideways size you up
through orange-rimmed lorgnettes.

Grandly plumed, they are full of disparagement
and treat the whole world with contempt.
Loud and quivering with rage, they strut away complaining
the food is always late, and never enough.

Stupid too and supercilious.
When the butcher comes, they'll tell the world at large
THEY HAVE THE GRAVEST DOUBTS
WHETHER THE LITTLE MAN REALLY KNOWS HIS
   BUSINESS.

Honey-bee

She's in overdrive. An inner spring propels
that dogged gathering, that persevering flight.
Among the thick dust of production lines
she zooms, an out-and-out Stakhanovite.

And quota after quota she will bear
back to the waxy darkness of the hive
with its swarming, crawling touchy-feeliness,
the whole thing geared to keep a queen alive.

Isn't she the perfect social animal?
No half-belief or existential doubt
impairs her absolute efficiency.
She is no drone, no licensed layabout.

Ants are the same. No pause for second thoughts,
no reservations and no turning back,
but driven onwards by a stubborn gene
with common outcomes on a common track.

These ardent, never-resting commonwealths –
insect Leviathans that wax and swell
without a whiff of teleology
beyond the filling of a honey-cell –

have blind compulsions that we cannot follow,
an etched imperative to do and die
for the common good, not knowing what it is;
self-sacrifice by sting, not knowing why.

Inchworm

Green upon green, and ravenous for green,
she inches forward after cellulose,
an undulating harvesting machine.

Programmed to scythe out any leaf that grows
within her range and stretch and loop and swing,
bent on the only mission that she knows –

her transformation into a flying thing,
a moth apotheosis in the sky,
the pupa-birth of eye and leg and wing

and so to propagate and multiply
through endless rounds of dual packaging –
grubs that can eat, imagoes that can fly.

She is no worm. This way of travelling
has convolutions that no worm can try.
Back legs slide up to where the front legs cling.

She measures out her body as she goes
by inches, loop after loop, meandering –
tiptoe and fall, then tiptoe, fall and close –

through mazes of the tree's broad mezzanine.
Against the foliage her body shows
a slow voracious motion, green upon green.

Newt

Fired-up he's not. No flame-proof salamander,
this damp amphibian fenny-pool recluse –
really he needs rebranding.

Even his given name has gone askew –
the Saxon eft-word carelessly adorned
with its indefinite article.

And, although crested, he is bog-plebeian,
pond-pursuivant, quartered in the mud.
For centuries he's made no mark –

except that, unprovoked, the Bard consigned
his eye, with other dubious ingredients,
to the Weird Sisters' bouillabaisse.

Still, he gets by. For instance, loss of leg
won't break his breast-stroke. Soon enough
it grows back, toes and all.

And all the while he's cleaning up the leeches
and slugs, in season, getting on with things
in his own quiet way.

So speak fair of the newt, and wish him well
in his unsung life and appetites
among dead leaves and stagnant pools.

Rat

Rat
is ubiquitous,
an ear that hears everything;
a plasma with volition;
a black economy.

Rat
is a shadow within a shadow;
a dark polis of duct and culvert.

Rat
is a sore that does not heal;
a scar from old wars.

Rat
is razzia and scourge.
Rat
is a horde.

Beware of those
who come silently.

They may smell
of the rat.

Starlings

For Matthew

In swollen clouds the starlings veer
and wheel and rise and swoop and sheer

in tight formations with a skill
owing nothing to mind or will

but immanent in all that makes
a starling and the tribe it takes.

Zoologists have all the facts
on how it musters and reacts;

the fold and camber of its wing;
its tilt and all its functioning.

The weight of skeleton is known,
and the porosity of bone.

They have the measure of the beak –
its outward thrust and how oblique.

They monitor the habitat;
and everything that goes with that –

migration, numbers, distribution,
reproduction, food, pollution.

For starling life in every phase
there is a copious data-base.

But/

But how the starling comes to be
remains an unsolved mystery –

The evolution of each cell
into nerve or claw or quill;

the implant in each starling brain
of sequences you could not train;

the instinct that impels that tight,
instantaneous, wheeling flight

of up and down and over-under
like a wave. We watch and wonder.

from *39 Ways of Looking* [2005]

Vincent's chair

He's put it down, the pipe, to take his brush
and touch up *Vincent* on the corner chest.
Perched on the rushes of the chair,
they tell you, do the pouch and pipe,
their owner can't be far away.

It's Vincent's own chair waiting patiently
on the tiled floor for him to finish off,
pocket the pipe and take his seat again
once the last strokes are dry. (That won't take long
in Arles' oven of a summer day.)

The *Ding an sich*. A right-of-insight claim
to all rush-bottomed kitchen chairs.
It's unassailable. *Look close,
it's what it is* the painter says,
and how it's meant to stay.

Elsewhere, his day may swirl
with sunflowers and cypresses.
But the kitchen chair's content to wait
for the wet paint to dry
and the old pipe to be put away.

Shamans

Under the rock at Drakensberg,
ochre dancers twine with fish
and herds of running antelope.
Possessed by spirits and familiars,
shamans arch their backs in pain.

Women stamp and clap their hands
to make the eland come.
The shamans fly and elongate.
They swim in water with an eel.
They bleed to bring the healing rain.

After the moon and stars have set
and the leopard's safe inside his cave,
with ash and earth the bushman paints
totem and fetish on the wall
to make the spirits rise again.

Listen. Below the rock you'll hear
the urgent drum and ritual
of man and spirit-animal
across ten thousand years,
vibrating in the lower brain.

Kyoto garden

The garden shrine of Ryoan-ji.
A seasonless parterre of sand
raked into enigmatic whorls
around the shores of islands-stones,
fastidious and monochrome.

Nothing here but by design –
the seeming motion of the sand
and seeming rise of island-stone
invite the eye to move
from rock to swirling comb

and back, and back again, until it finds
a point of equilibrium,
a harbourage of calm.
Around the whiteness of the sand
a wall of ancient loam

holds its possession tight and tells
that nothing good comes without sanctuary,
that it's the frame that frees the space within,
that even flawless images require
a shelter and a home.

Pen-y-ghent

So to the nab of Pen-y-Ghent
where moor's impounded in a maze of walls
and landscape speaks in accents that I know –
a tongue of scars and rakes and becks
straight from the Norse. A land of spur and knoll,

rough pasture on the valley side,
a cold wind scouring over scarp
from Ribblehead. Here is my own;
my latitude and dialect,
my discourse and parole.

From this bleak Sinai the moors roll out
austere and puritan and fall
in tussock, stone and reed
sodden to the valley floors
down gill and swallow-hole.

If there's illusion here,
it's deeply rooted in the bone
and ineradicable.
This is native heath and home,
meridian and pole.

Winter day above Dent

High in this circle of familiar hills,
mind fuses with their stretch and rising,
moulds to their wrap and folding,
and the sweep of scar and ghyll;

and down where Helm's Knott swells,
stubbled with heather, latches on
to the great Fault splitting Lakes from Dales,
where Pennines butt up against Lakeland fell.

All unity, the valley's scoop appears
from this vantage point, but underground
the strata are at odds: one step and you're out
by a hundred million years.

Swift becks lay bare the skeleton;
disclose the fractures and the shattered bones
of breccia and conglomerate –
the twist and grind and shudder of convulsion.

But in the dale a daub of green and brown
covers the sync- and anti-cline.
Its soft contours mantle the rend and fission
which aeons of wind and rain have whittled down.

Now all is calm. The fossil shells
And coral colonies lie silent
under upland farms. Deep seams of limestone
bed down quietly with shale.

Sedge glows in the setting winter sun
like fox's fur: long capes of shadow fall
From drystone walls: ice underfoot
warns that the short bright day will soon be done.

Haikus for a summer day

Black on shorn fields lie
litters, plump, of new-baled hay.
Sun glints on their skin.

At noon, a great roar.
Fighters spattering upland
with terrified sheep.

At the river-fall
boys loll in shade where willows
furrow the water.

* * *

Daylight is fading.
Edge of shadow unhouses
sun from the treetops.

Swifts wheel and sabre,
cutting the clouds to ribbons
of silver and grey.

Dusk brings out chafers.
Deep-throated tractors harvest
by headlight and moon.

Open the atlas

Open the atlas. Here the world is calm
and clear and amenable,
the continents all lined up to appear
on the same apron stage;
the globe smoothed down
into a planisphere.

The map lies docile on the page,
all frontiers fixed, the oceans still.
No earthquakes or eclipse.
Sahara, forest, ice,
fjord and Everest
all soft under the fingertips.

For sure the frontiers will not hold.
Time will bleach out
imperial colours.
Catastrophe will topple
contours, kings, caudillos,
ayatollahs.

Yet for a moment taste
the quiet of illusion,
the continents at rest,
entirely still,
oceans becalmed,
the nations motionless.

from *The Silence of Green* [2007]

Lebensraum

Spring goads and green worlds drive for *lebensraum*.
Roots arm and mobilise and launch an underground
and blind assault down unmarked corridors,
their targets an uncharted hinterland
of troughs and hollows with obscure horizons.

Clandestine, silent foragers fan out
through dark compressions of the netherscape
probing its folds and fingering its lie.
They infiltrate and tap and scan
For flecks of iron, zinc locked up in clay.

Networks spread out to hold the province down
and haul back sap and spoil through labyrinths
of cell and valve and vent and stem
to confluence in uplift to the sun –
commitment into xylem.

The Silence of Xylem

Xylem's the green world's Grand Trunk Road,
the fibre super-highway piping sap
from unlit depots up through bole
to tree-top termini. Plants stretch up tall
to make a thoroughfare.

And yet there's not a whisper to be heard.
No resonance or rushing in the tubes,
or gurgling in the long capillaries,
or tremolo as sap threads through
the narrowest branches.

Out of foliage pour endless molecules.
The air is thick with them but there is still no sound.
Xylem conceals great silences like that of lymph
or other noiseless interstitial fluids, or corpuscles,
or the unheard motion of bacteria.

It doesn't know when to stop

The green world doesn't know when to stop.
Left to itself it would go on and on
advancing root and rhizome,
cloning weed and water hyacinth,
till everything was clogged up tight with greenery.
Only the bugs and drought and ice withstand
a great global greenhouse.
Already cooler latitudes are stiff
with pine's incalculable foliage.

For sure it doesn't need our ministration.
Witness its silence and the way
it stands apart, expecting nothing from us,
attending to its own green destiny
of growth and replication and decay
and answering directly to the sun.
It doesn't need our laboured intervention,
the way we have to turn it to our use
and bind it tightly to our own survival.

No Mangos in Tibet

Passionless, devoid of thought,
the great green world lacks any sense
of what's enough or what's proportionate.
It lives by sun and soil and chance,

Unchecked, it spreads till aquifers run dry,
grows tall till gravity declines
to lend a further hand; drives all the way
down to impenetrable stone.

It takes excess of sun and absent rain
to place it in parenthesis.
Heat cancels, drought disowns,
ice brings paralysis.

It has to make the best of what it gets
under the edict of climatic law.
No mangos dangle in Tibet.
No giant sitkas rise in Arkansas.

Welwitschia to Bristlecone

Squat, dishevelled baglady of Namibia, O
you really are in quite a mess.
Your two and only underblankets sprawl
in tatters on the ground.
Your tongue is always hanging out
in eager expectation of the hour
when fog comes rolling up the coastal strip
and you can get your first drink of the day.

You've been around for ever.
Way, way before Magellan sailed his skimpy caravel
into the Benguela drift, you hunkered down
in this far-from-prepossessing pitch.
Your ancestors date back to the Jurassic,
each fossil generation scratching out
the same bare living from the wilderness.
You keep your head by lying low.

The same goes for the bristlecone,
another ancient down-at-heel survivor.
High in the Rockies where the ice-winds blow,
it clocks millennia by sitting tight.
Half-naked through its rags of bark
it isn't beautiful at all.
Just very old, like you, and with no choice;
having to make the best of what it's got.

Bonsai at Wisley

Distinct among the showpiece patios,
two well-drilled lines of bonsai constitute
a kind of pantheon or sacred grove.

They have the grace of cameos,
each slender silhouette displaying
calm and delicate adroitness.

Diminutive they may be, but convey
no sense of anything gone missing
in reduction to the miniature.

Who can belittle artistry which keeps
such faith with form and archetype,
and shows such skill in timber made petite?

Ages of Oak

Limbs of adolescent oak, high on chlorophyll and sap,
can't help but make their restless presence felt,
no matter how unsure they are
of their ground and standing.

Green-gowned in summer, oak is mandarin,
all pomp and parasol and pride of place.
Unhurriedly, it takes all day to paint
the sunlight with a wash of shade.

Stoic, umber, autumn oak,
full of rooks, is in receivership.
Each day, relentless winds come round
to wheel away its chattels.

Antlered, geriatric oak,
blackened, full of scab and gnarl
and hollowed out, has years of stooping
leafless in its last eclipse.

The ambition of Ivy

Ivy simply doesn't know where to stop –
it's all excess and appetite
and unrestrained ambition.
Left to its own devices it would latch
on to every possible vertical
and go right to the top.
And spread out too, taking the whole frontage
given half a chance.
And it's so flagrant, making absolutely
no attempt to hide its tracks.
And, worst of all,
it gets away with it!

Ode to the Artichoke

The artichoke, stand-offish, over-clad,
is bristling, sealed and taut.
Only the fiercest hunger could have brought
its early fanciers to tunnel out
the tender heart from under all that coat
of thistle, scale and spike.

Neruda once conjectured that it hoped
to join a plant militia.
For other *aficionados* it evokes
not martial, but lascivious images
as they peel off its green veils, one by one.
Not soldier-boy, but stripper.

(Hear Merrie Andrew Borde who warned
that artichokes, like onions, *provoke*
a man to venéryous actes.
The voice of hard experience. Unfrocked,
he ran a brothel on the side
while writing Tudor Baedekers.)

Eating the artichoke is always quite
a performance. Bract after leathery bract discarded
down to the bunny-fluff of the choke
(all spit and feathers if you get it wrong)
on your lingering, deliberate way
to its finally unguarded heart.

Zeus was as keyed up as they come
in his wooing in the Peloponnese
of Cynara whom he wished to gormandize.
Would she become a goddess please? Oh yes.
But when she flounced off, bored, back home,
he zipped her tightly in an artichoke.

And what should Norma Jeane become,
in 1949 in Monterey,
but the *Queen of Artichokes*?
A future goddess she who, faced with any god,
would never hesitate it seems to shed
all of her covering.

An Aloe in Natal

Behind a high wire fence, green lawns recline
in a white suburban comfort zone
blue-pooled and pink with bougainvillea.
The fence is razored and electrified
to keep what's undesired away.

But even so an aloe's muscled in –
a trespasser with serious attitude
which kicks its legs up at the laundry-maid
and menaces the gardener with knives
as he pads off home when the sun goes down.

It came alone and got to stay,
making itself at home in the kitchen yard
where all the junk gets tipped well out of sight –
the broken telephone, the seized-up radio,
the tandem short of handlebars.

It's a plant that knows how to look after itself –
not one to cross or tangle with.
See that rosette of lances and the fronds like saws?
Aloe's a logo for a fetichist
or emblem for a penitentiary.

Moor song

Here is my element.
The lift and swell
and lip and lie.
The stretch of sky
over the hills.
The way moor folds;
the way it breaks
into a run of ghylls;
the way it falls;
the way the wide fells
hold the eye and all
is clear and still.

Song of wool

River water, swift and soft,
rising up through valley mist,
swelling thread of warp and weft.

Elemental wool. Its smell
stoppering nostrils – rank and full;
carcassed in a canvas bale.

Tireless metronome of loom.
Hammering and deafening crash
of steel-tipped shuttle slamming home.

Young boy on a blackened floor
watching as the broad cloth grows,
listening as the steam clouds pour

out hissing to the cobbled yard
where he'll linger with the fine
rusting things that mills discard.

Consolations

Solomon's seal
A double row of pendant pearls –
or is it white socks on a washing line? –
announce beside the shed in spring
the flowering of her Solomon's seal.

Each year she grumbles things have got behind.
The garden's slow. There's so much to be done.
But she's always pleased to see this plant again,
its long spray bending to the job in hand.

For her it is a righteous sign of hope
that all things in due season get renewed;
and that the past may yet be made
once more of service, and in decent shape.

Sweet William
She'd have Sweet William for her funeral.
It once was someone's favourite that she loved,
and that's the sense of it she's kept for years.

Not as pot-pourri or pretence of everlasting flowers,
but as a gaudy, living coronal to honour
every season, not excluding death.

Gorse and heather
Yellow gorsebrake in the clough,
purple heather on the moor,
rough grass by the reservoir,
gritstone outcrop on the scarp.

This/

This, her childhood; this is where
the steps of memory are good and wide
and where her waking dreams are made,
the slow days when she'll sit and stare.

Mahonia, chaenomeles
Aging, everything on hold,
looking out on snow she sees
mahonia, chaenomeles,
winter crimson, winter gold.

Beacons shining through the cold
warm her spirit, give her ease:
mahonia, chaenomeles,
winter crimson, winter gold.

Day by day their buds unfold
colours which face down the freeze:
mahonia, chaenomeles,
winter crimson, winter gold.

Body growing stiff and old,
let her take delight from these:
mahonia, chaenomeles,
winter crimson, winter gold.

My private island

Shelving to turbid sea, my private island's
barely perceptible at any tide, its marsh and dune
shrouded in haze; an interim estate
where sedge and marram intertwine and bond

with silt and shell to form an element
which force of waves could quickly overwhelm.
Cartographers would draw the line
at calling it dry land.

An under-surveyed and low-lying sill
is what it is, on a delta's edge,
made up of sediment washed down
from restless hinterlands of scour and till;

a place of transience – and yet
its mine alone, and private, and apart.

Nuance

Those who like things black and white
can't stomach prisms which let stray
shining strands of coloured light
play upon their certainty.

Plain-vanilla zealots wince
at polychrome confections made
of mango, strawberry and quince.
Or passion-fruit, for heaven's sake!

Awkward angles stub the toes
of those who wear a party shoe.
Novelty offends the eyes
of those who think as others do.

Thank God for nuance with its blade
whittling away at stereotype.
Thank God for those who see the shades
which free from choke of black and white.

What they settled for

Advised in spring of the peril of flood
they settled for a few short blasts on a whistle.

Advised in summer of the threat of famine
they settled for a dietary solution.

Advised in autumn of incipient plague
they settled for a thirty-minute talk on 'Epidemiology made
    easy'.

Advised in winter of horrific death
they settled for a part-time telephonist with a diploma in
    funerary etiquette.

Going critical

There are words which must be handled with great care.

Some verbs are radioactive and ignite spontaneously:
it is imperative to take their heat away.

Brought suddenly together, conjunctions can react.
A clause may be enough to take a city out.

Adverbs, too, can be incendiary.
Even a comma can prove flammable.

Can you hear – it may be very faint –
the dull throb of a safety monitor?

If not, then close the book and leave
as quickly as you can.

Extracts from *The Maze: a daydream in five cantos* [2009]

[The poem, of over 700 lines, is an imaginative excursion
into poetic landscape, with calls on Pope, Wordsworth and
other poets.
Canto One opens as follows.]

Late in the year, one morning I awoke
and found myself shut in on every side
by high and thorny edges with a cloak

of thick fog everywhere. There was no hide
or hut, no sound, no voice; nothing to show
location or bearing; nothing to guide –

only a narrow alley where, with slow
steps, I moved between the hedges, feeling
my way, the mist swirling, my courage low.

As day wore on, the haze dispersed, revealing
long lines of foliage with intersections
and dead ends. I knew then I was dealing

with a maze ...

[*Canto Five* ends as follows with an exchange with Ezra Pound.]

You asked me why I bothered to persist
with terza rima. It's the power I said
of a well-tuned engine. No ventriloquist

free verse has got the throttle or the cred.
Cadence is subtle, but can be illusory
and roll into the sand. Rhyme stays in the head,

and/

and stacks; avoids just-what-you-choosery.
The poet shook his head and went off fast
muttering darkly about graft and usury,

abuse of Dante, and my dubious past
and unpropitious future. I resigned
myself to stoical endurance. *Blast*

the maze, but I must take it as I find
it and make do! I cried, as I set out
to stake my ground where I was most inclined,

and build my wall, my tower, my redoubt.

from *The Intruders* [2010]

Just tell them what they want to hear

Fox warns *Don't try to make a mark*
on stately minds. It doesn't work.
Just tell them what they want to hear.

You get no credit when you show
their pedestal is insecure.
They see you as a mutineer.

And keep off things they do not know
or topics where they feel unsure.
Just tell them what they want to hear –

that green means stop and red means go,
that sour is sweet and sweet is sour,
that near is far and far is near;

that more is less and less is more,
that half a dozen make a score.
Just tell them what they want to hear.

Turning a blind eye

Turning a blind eye
is a simple courtesy says Fox,
when stumbling on unfortunate mistakes
in business or in politics.

There isn't always time to cover tracks.
Unguarded letters, careless signatures
leave trails which never fail to lure
snoopers and impertinents.

In such a case, to volunteer
what otherwise would stay unseen
may cause unnecessary pain,
and seem, at best, ungenerous.

Per contra, wise discretion can cement
bonds of mutual abetting.
Don't tell me that you've never made
a good thing from equivocation.

I take the high ground and reply
Not so. I've done no other than acquit
myself with honour in the public interest.
I'd always bring foul play to light.

Fox doubts my memory and leers
But what about your careful hand
in all those Answers given to Parliament
designed to cast no light at all?

O that was politics I say.
The gentle art of non-transparency.
Time-honoured Party games of hide-and-seek
which everyone learns how to play.

How good he was!

Gurus of the avant-garde agreed
his canvases were strangely bare but said
how good he was at doing what he did

with strings of zeros on a faint grey grid.
Some dismissed him as a knucklehead,
but gurus of the avant-garde agreed

a style so spare was certain to succeed,
and spoke of an artistic watershed.
How good he was at doing what he did!

A few groaned *Arte povera indeed!*
and damned the canvases as *all but dead*,
but gurus of the avant-garde agreed

the market would be very quick to feed
on strings of zeros once the word had spread
how good he was at doing what he did.

And so it proved. The dealers worked up speed,
guessing their take would rise with every bid,
since gurus of the avant-garde agreed
how good he was at doing what he did.

Trust the engineers

Sick of the gimcrack scaffolding
of bankers, party freaks, and hacks,
from now I'll place my trust in engineers

well trained to take true measurements
and make things work, and calibrate,
and size things to perfection –

canny turbine-makers, those
who know the codes of shear and stress,
high priests of pressure vessels, valves,

and all who master wires and gears,
who bridge and mine and tunnel, warranting
the last word in precision,

who deal in strength and weight and height,
and know materials inside out,
and how far you can go.

These are the people that I'll trust –
the ones to whom I'll look with confidence
to underpin and buttress and embed

and anchor all securely.
Wise illuminati of foundations.
Missioners of steel and terra firma.

From *Five Songs for Sarah*

i. Marmalade

Here is a bowl of bitter oranges
like those we've seen in hundreds on the ground,
windfalls, in public gardens in Seville.

And bags of sugar which could once have come
from sweet stalks cut on your father's farm
in the humid cane-fields of Natal.

And here's experience too, from which we've learned
how best to balance our ingredients
and blend them carefully until they've set.

And here are jars which soon will bottle up
the marmalade we share and share alike.
We know it's good. We know that it will keep

until it's needed, cool and still,
mature, approaching golden, and delectable.

ii. Wicken jelly

Since autumn is now our season,
let it be glorious and magnified
by all your *cucurbitae* exotics –
Turk's turban pumpkins, serpentine courgettes –
and at Wicken let us go and pick
hips and sloes and blackberries.

There's no call to be elegiac.
We'll take preserving pans and make
the pickles and the sweet dark jams
we like to label, seal and keep
in our coolest larder, knowing we provide
for every season, sweet and sour together.

Return to the Pennines

Dusk brings me to my native hills
where limestone skeleton breaks through
a sodden moorland skin.

I watch long flanks of shadow darken
what's already drab and dark. I walk
where mosses huddle in deep fissures.

It's not geology that's brought me back,
or fossils, or an itch to hear
pebbles clatter down swallow-holes.

Nor am I after rushes or cotton-grass.
I'm not moved by a collector's urge
to fill botanic jars with specimens.

And I haven't come for the sake of listening to
the grate and clang of Viking names,
the kelds and thwaites and riggs and gills.

I've come because the sprawling Pennine script
is written deep inside me, and
in truth I read it every single day,

knowing the moorland trails by heart,
knowing my hands were meant from birth
to raise well-stacked cairns and strong drystone walls.

from *Lyrics from the Periodic Table* [2011]

A song for oxygen

With which we have no choice but to sustain
lifelong intimate relations.
From our first lift of lung and searching cry
to our last moments of relinquishing
it's closer than love, and longer-lasting.
And not just us but everything that breathes
shares that long dependency,
that lifetime and unchangeable submission.

The inertia of argon

Argon is entirely self-sufficient
and keeps itself to itself.
It needs no business partner for its atoms
and turns whatever offer down
of a share in whatever action.

Left to its own low-key devices
it would hang unnoticed round
some sleepy corner of the atmosphere –
accumulating – ye-e-s – but not too fast,
and going absolutely nowhere.

Placed in packaging it sits quite still,
minding its own remote affairs,
keeping things in silent quarantine,
keeping them entirely undisturbed,
and nothing – nothing – happens.

Stardust calcium

Of which we have
a kilogram inside us,
stardust atoms
blown out in the flux
of countless supernovas,
briefly now installed
in teeth and skeleton,
all certain in the end
to break away from
this short-lived coalition,
this purely temporary
embodiment in bone.

The charms of zinc

Commonplace, uncolourful,
conventionally tainted by
association with damp table-tops
in bistros and the like,
zinc seems destined to evoke
nothing but grey metallic thoughts.

And yet it's pretty in the coat
it spangles over sheeted steel,
crystal patterns glinting
as the cutter strikes and throws
a golden wrap of sparks
over its thin shoulders.

And in audacious calamine
it dresses up in shocking pink
to dab and chasten and face down
the hot gaze of the sun,
and turn young kids with chicken pox
into a slapdash comedy show.

Inside us, too, the zinc-y molecules
are always in a flutter,
sweeping round the body's galleries
in a non-stop bustle of catalysis,
keeping our proteins up to scratch
and looking really good.

Adieu to mercury

Beaded sweat of cinnabar it is,
a toxic near-vermilion
bleeding drops of brilliant silver.
Alchemists saw liquid gold mock them in its glitter.

For Greeks, its scurry spoke their courier-god,
his sandals trimmed with fetching little wings.
All China's rivers shone with mercury
in the jewelled tomb of Emperor Chi'n.

Smeared on chancred roués, it was prized
as the morning-after cure of choice,
filling a highly profitable niche
in unfastidious surgeries.

For ages it was billed as the liveliest act
in the pantomime of elements,
dodging, tumbling, racing, skidding,
jumping through the hoop of its own meniscus.

But now it's slipped right out of fashion.
Incinerators waft mercurial fumes
from morbid batteries and dead thermometers.
Redundant dental fillings vaporise in the fires of crematoria.

from *A sequence from the Cyclades* [2012]

Islands rise at dawn

Islands rise at dawn.
The morning star hangs over
a pale wash of sea.

Dawn is the best time.
Stars are fading fast below
the lap of light's tide.

Tamarisk brushes
softly across a shutter
as the wind rises.

Sun takes the hillside.
Windows catch its early gold.
On the sea, jewels.

High wind on Serifos

High wind on Serifos
drives wisps of cloud to Crete
and puts all flags in business.

North walls quake and shudder.
Even the lichen has to hold on tight
when the *meltémi* blows.

Its sound is everywhere.
It howls down alleyways and treats
all unheld shutters to a wild percussion.

It rubs against the sea's nap
and makes a mockery of sheltered waters.
Halyards lash at masts and decks.

None can leave the island now
until the high wind drops its claim
to the high-crested Aegean.

Possession

The shore's too open to possession
in these fragmentary islands.
First piracy, and now the package deals
are over-running them.
Not only that, but the brutal sea's
relentlessly exploring and abrading
their excrescences and perforations
with its rough salt tongue.

Legend too hangs heavy on these islands.
It buzzes like bees in the thyme.
It runs like geckos round the walls.
It holds their landscape in its hawk's eye.
It draws so strongly they can keep nothing away.
From the start, they offered stepping-stones.
Now they have landing strips to speed
conquest by their worshippers.

Dusk in Naxos

It's dusk in Naxos and along the quay
candles flicker on the cafe tables.
Waiters lure and hustle passers-by
with a flourish of their establishment's
all-too-predictable *katálogos*:
moussaka and *stifadho* and *souvlaki*.

There's dancing later, but *rembetika*'s
already getting wildly amplified
by sound-men fixing speakers on the stage.
Evening cool has brought the widows out
to sit and watch the flow of the *plateía*.
Children chase around in pools of light.

No sign tonight of a tragic view of life,
no glimpse of any fascistic ghost
or debt-collector lurking in the shadows.
Yet all the widows and the waiters know
that thread of summer can wear thin
and, in a colder season, may unravel.

Winds on Naxos

A brisk wind blowing from the east
ruffles the sea off Naxos.
Trim your sails and you could reach
Corinth on a breeze like this.

Wind in Naxos from the north
scatters jasmine, litters patios
with petals of bougainvillea.
A steady blow and you'd be down to Crete.

West wind sidling in from Paros
flaps awning on the waterfront.
Try to catch it as it heads away
to a mooring in Limassol.

Hot wind blowing from the south
shrivels the citron leaves of Naxos.
South winds red with Libyan sand
could sweep you up to Samothrace.

A ring of islands

A ring of islands which unites
shrine and saint with rock and sea.
True believers come to find
ecstatic landscapes of the mind
in bold centralities of white
circumscribed by depths of blue.

A ring of islands which persists
in pulling drawstrings good and tight
round pining hearts of exiled acolytes
and stirring, as they softly browse
on Greek in distant libraries,
the viscera of Hellenists.

Extract from *Night Train to Utopia and other tales* [2013]

[The lawyers, religious zealots, hippies and others who board
the Night Train are utterly self-centred. Their only glimpse
of Utopia leaves them in deep shock. Some make their way
via desert to a war zone, which may be their final destination.
These are the opening verses of the 600-line saga. The
volume contains three other substantial narrative poems –
The withering of vines, *The horse plague*, and *After the Pied Piper*.]

Never advertised, the night train runs
a private service to Utopia.
You'll find no schedule of departures.

Never on open sale, couchettes
are offered randomly to those who call.
You take them when you can.

The booking clerk will not inquire
what sort of baggage you intend to bring.
You'll not be questioned on your mental health.

He'll have no information on hotels
or what to wear. He'll simply say
that things are taken care of on arrival.

The train leaves from a station in the suburbs
where its dingy rolling stock's put in the shade
by busy, brightly-coloured shuttles

gliding smoothly in and out,
taking the brisk and purposeful
from animated place to place.

It's/

It's standing at a platform to the side,
where tall weeds push up through the track
and rails lie bent and derelict.

Its livery is brown and puce
and what might once have passed for gold.
A door, half-open, warns *Défense* ...

By the barrier, there's a person hawking
a range of creature comforts for the journey –
earplugs, masks, inhalers, stomach pills,

and reading-matter such as almanacs
of moon and tide, and horoscopes,
and handbooks on survival.

A salesman's pushing policies which offer
cover on demand for memory loss,
and life insurance with a no-claim bonus.

The long-amortised engine gets up steam,
gasping and hissing from defective valves.
Soot drifts down from its rusty stack.

The destination boards begin to flash
This train is ready to depart.
Expect delays of almost any length....

from *Satires and Legacies* [2014]

Extract from *Purdue's Tale*

[Jonah Purdue leads a quiet bachelor life until he encounters
the private-finance SKEWED company which plans to staff
its care homes with young offenders from SKEWED-run
jails. When Purdue blows the whistle he faces an
establishment cover-up. The narrative runs to over 500 lines
in 14 parts.]

1. Purdue buttonholes
a stranded traveller

Under the stopped hands of a disused clock
two stranded travellers sit disconsolate
beside the metal blinds of closed boutiques.
The coach they've long been waiting for is caught

in freezing fog that's gripped the motorway
and locked it in a ten-mile traffic jam –
a solid block of fuming misery.
It could be hours before it comes.

The younger one is wearing standard gear –
black leather jacket, trainers, faded jeans.
He'd hoped to join a stag-night swilling beer.
The hold-up means he's missing all the fun.

The older man has heavy corduroys,
stout shoes, dark sweater, anorak with hood.
The transport snarl-up means he'll lose a day
of watching birdlife from a wetland hide.

The/

The movement board is blank. The café's shut.
The booking clerks have left their darkened posts.
The terminal's last coach is pulling out
to the ribald chant of raucous wedding guests.

The two are on their own now in the hall.
The watchman's dimmed the glare of concourse lights.
They have no option but to sit or sprawl
and drowse or pace about to pass the night.

The young man fiddles with a hand-held game.
The older puzzles over crossword clues.
From time to time he grunts and moves his arm
as if he's going to rise. The minutes pass.

He waits till he can catch the other's eye
then coughs and puts his paper down and speaks.
Excuse me. I should like to say hello.
My name is Jonah Purdue. It'll take

all night before the coach arrives and so
perhaps you'd like to hear of something strange
that happened to me not so long ago.
Don't worry. I am not at all deranged

but I've suffered a disturbing episode
and sharing it will help to ease my mind.
It's all about a company called SKEWED".
The young man nodded and the tale began.

A Master Chef with grand designs

Here is a Master Chef with grand designs.
His kitchens throb with power and heat.
He knows the arts of seasoning.
He has a way with sauce and spice.
His highly-coloured menus catch the eye.
His recipes are full of bite.

Cuisine for him is all about invention.
His best ingredient – surprise;
his second best – concealment.
His *cod mornay,* drugged hard with cheese,
could well be dogfish in disguise.
His *faux-filet* is falser than it seems.

He glories in an embonpoint
which fleshes out his bonhomie.
His humour's rich and never undersold.
He likes to laugh a lot and when he laughs
his eyes sink into many folds.
And yet they're not quite lost to sight.

The laughs grow louder
and the folds grow deeper
but still there's something glittering inside –
a needlepoint, a tiny aperture
receiving and absorbing,
assessing and recording.

The/

The jokes roll on.
The table's in a fit.
He toasts the clientele and feeds the mood
with little quips. He's smart and droll.
Shoulders are heaving. Smooth jowls shake.
He knows that's how the best champagne gets sold.

At other times he stands quite still
and when he speaks his voice is low
so all those round him can't just catch
his drift, or keep up with the flow.
But should his sous-chefs spoil the dish, he'll swear
he put them fully in the know.

Behind the many-layered smile
lie boundless depths of vanity.
He's sure he is the prince and president
of all concoctions. And the life and soul
of any worthwhile party.
He quivers with ambition.

His stock is rising. He's a *succès fou*.
He plans to build a franchise nation-wide
with self-promotion wall-to-wall
and top spots for his menus and his name.
Those with the sharpest eyes for fame
are placing orders for his *table d'hôte*.

There was a state that lost its head

There was a state that lost its head.
It lost its head and then its heart
It lost its heart and then its words,
the words it lived by from the start.

There was a state that lost its words,
the words it needed for its heart.
It lost the heart that made the head.
Without a head, it fell apart.

[In the volume *Satires and Legacies*, the poem *Inheritance* introduces narratives on Francis Bacon, William Penn, Captain Cook, Edward Jenner and Thomas Clarkson. The poem *A few words of praise* concludes the series.]

Inheritance

Good or bad
there's no escaping it.

Life from first to last depends
on bonds we've inherited –

securities that have no date
of expiration or release.

Our histories are rich with evidence
of balances that linger –

debts requiring service, and facilities on which
it would be witless not to draw.

* * *

A few words of praise

for alpha legacies which we inherit
for slow-burn faith which tolerates the rest
for those who see abuse and cannot bear it
for those who face crass ignorance and persist
for all who seek the best and share it.

Three poems from *Exchanges with Angel*

So late in life

Angel comes up looking stern.
He carps

So late in life and still you lack
a fully worked-out personal agenda.
You can't stay 50-50 all the way –
a sort of everlasting floating voter.

I say *I'm from a sceptical tradition*
taught early to watch out for self-deceit.
I take belief with grains of reservation.
I seed my hope with doubts which may prove certain.

Angel calls that specious. He retorts

How typical of a liberal education!
At root you're idle and have failed to read
your Aristotle or Boethius.
Or if you have, you've closed your ears to meaning.

What of your inner strength? Your power of reason?
Self-knowledge? Self-control?
Your sense of ultimate concern?

Sporadic I reply.
It fluctuates with mood and circumstance.
I don't keep score.

Angel scowls and says that those who know
what's good for them don't fail to take
at least one daily philosophic reading.

A warning

Angel turns up in his guardian mode
and warns:

*Remember: stay alert and watch your back
for warped fanatics who can hit you hard
and sharp-tongued dogmas hunting in a pack.*

*It pays you to be constantly on guard.
The wretched earth can scarcely hold
the corpses they have buried.*

In lower key he adds:

*Of course –
in time –
you may be forced –
like half the globe –
to run like mad.*

To which I judge
at present
there is nothing
useful
to be said.

Full and final settlement

Says Angel *Sign here on the dotted line*
in full and final settlement.

Surely I cry *my claim's for more than that –*
a decimal point, a lengthy row of noughts
and a lonely figure ONE
with no denomination?

But that he says *is what you're going to get –*
your due share of a vast accumulation.

At this time there can be no certain value.
It's a kind of trust.

from *Homecoming by Microlight* [2015]

Resurrection at Dent

In rain-swept Dent, the day of resurrection
won't look like Stanley Spencer's sunny Cookham.
No bright Thames Valley light will shine on heaving graves.
There'll be nothing in the setting to suggest
a nice reviving cup of tea

and maybe a regatta on the river
once everything's been straightened out
and the tombstones put back neatly.
No sense of a brass band standing by
to play Jerusalem, or the Old Hundredth.

In Dent, it will be sombre and reserved.
The weather will be Pennine, with a mist
descending on the churchyard, its memorials
shrouded as the farming dead arise.
Sheep will move through everything like ghosts.

Pouring rain will put the damper on
triumphal choruses of hallelujah
or uplifting recitals of the Beatitudes.
The most you might expect to hear will be
a muttering of shorter psalms.

At a given signal, the whole band, mud on their feet,
will file down to the flatlands by the river
and, crossing the local Jordan in good order,
toil up the steep flanks of the dale to heaven,
hailing kin in dialect, or Norse.

Beginning of *Steel-capped PR*

[A satire on the PR industry of over 190 lines in six parts.]

From the muddle in my bedside drawer
a crumpled ticket tumbles out.
Uncertain what the ticket's for

I hold it closer to the light
and find my eye drawn to a gap
where panelling has come apart.

I press. A click. A door slides back
to show a spacious entrance hall,
a *Welcome* plaque, a moving stair

rising with a gentle hum,
soft music in the atmosphere.
A voice intones *So glad you've come!*

I'm swept up on the moving stair
to an atrium of chrome and glass
and step off on a marble floor

beside an electronic screen
with an urgent cursor racing on
repeatedly in red and green.

A swoosh of red proclaims a class
on *How to place the blame;* then green
zips by with *How to sell the pass!!* –

with/

with exclamation marks in red.
Then – green again – a seminar
on *Engineering disrepute.*

It seems I've reached the fountain-head
of a firm called *Snarlings.* On the wall
an ice-blue neon logo reads:

*World-leaders in **Steel-capped PR**.*

Out of sight

Alone in towns, he couldn't find,
of all the many doors,
one that was right.

Adrift, he spoke to passers-by
who took one sideways look and hurried off.
There was no kindness in the street.

He searched in skips for this and that.
He thought discarded magazines
might tell him things that he'd forgot.

He'd linger hours by public offices
until policemen moved him on,
sometimes gently; sometimes not.

Believe me. People often stopped to say
he should be found – they weren't sure how –
some place of refuge or retreat

where, calmed, he might conveniently stay
quite safe, quite still,
and out of sight.

from *Brief Encounters* [2016]

Willy Brandt comes for breakfast, 1967

To Rome with George Brown for a rendezvous
of statesmen international.
Unwisely we've been pressed to stay
in promised five-star luxury
at our jewel of an Embassy.

A problem comes up right away.
A faulty line means outside calls
will ring on just two telephones
of which Phone One's by George Brown's bed –
unstoppable unless Phone Two
is picked up quickly in the hall.
It's Sunday, says the Ambassador.
No prospect of repair today.

For you to handle states the knight,
by now in dressing-gown. *Good night!*
And so for me the five-star treat
means hours spent slumped beside Phone Two
in the Villa's draughty vestibule.
At five I sleep. There's been no call.

I give a knock for George at eight,
reminding him that Willy Brandt
is due for breakfast here at nine –
no chance a German will be late!
And sure enough on the dot of nine
the doorbell rings. I show him in.

No sign of host but through a door
appears a rear view of George Brown,
his broad beam struggling as he tries
to urge his trousers into shape.
Appalled, I swiftly shut the door.
Apologies Herr Brandt I say.
I fear there'll be a slight delay.

A muffled sound – a growl, a curse.
It seems the trousers are engaged
in serious resistance still.
A broad grin spreads on Willy's face.
Don't worry friend. I've seen much worse!

Willy Brandt was West German Foreign Minister 1966-69. He and
George Brown (British Foreign Secretary 1966-68) attended a
meeting of the Socialist International in Rome in January 1967. At
a breakfast meeting at the Residence of the British Ambassador,
Brown urged Brandt's support for British entry into the EEC.

Greeting Monty, 1967

I'm to greet Monty, coming here
to bend the Foreign Office ear
on how to set the world to rights.

One who went through World War Two
and knows his Monty, jokes *He'll make you think
it's really <u>you</u> he's come to see.*

*He'd look a soldier in the eye,
and for a moment make him feel
essential to the infantry.*

*He'd single some man out and say
'Now let me ask you what <u>you</u> do.'*
I laugh. *He'll not be asking <u>me</u>!*

The car arrives. That famous face!
A flash-back to El Alamein!
Field-Marshal, please do come this way!

He's in no hurry, looks around
in all directions, wants to know
And why is that? or *When and where?*

We reach the grandeur of the final Stair
with its florid murals of Britannia,
its heavily symbolic dome,

and minatory *Silence*, large and grim,
her finger firmly on her lips.
(Let's hope he doesn't ask me why!)

Before this grand imperial scene
he pauses, looks me in the eye, and says
(I can't say that I wasn't warned)

Now let me ask you what <u>you</u> *do* ...

On not meeting Ronald Reagan, 1991

You wait they promise. *It's the biggest deal.*
An hour or two you'll get to see
a superman of destiny – the greatest!
I ask them – *Yes, but who?*
Right now, it seems, they're not allowed to tell.

But then excitement as the word goes round
first whispered, then crescendo – *Say!*
You've heard I guess? Incredible!
It's Ronald! Ronald!
Ronald's on his way!

I pause. My mind goes quickly to
a wave and smile I've seen a thousand times.
What more's to see?
The well-worn smile? The hand on heart?
The winning way?

It's Ronald or the Golden Gate.
Sorry I say *I just can't stay.*

from *The Wranglers and other poems* [2017]

7. Corruption

Fox thinks corruption is too harsh a word
for handy things like bribes which oil
so many wheels and breed a sense
of mutual advantage.

He sees them as a frank exchange of gifts
in which a contract may be matched
by some quite small emolument,
a minuscule percentage.

And where he muses *is the harm in that?*
Provided things are tacit, undeclared
and wholly imperceptible,
I lose no beauty sleep.

Angel contradicts. *All bribes mean someone*
somewhere has been ditched.
Not that they'll ever know it
sniggers Fox –

if all goes well.

11. *A hundred things to do before you die!*

The weekend colour mag proposes
A hundred things to do before you die!
Good Lord! you think. *I'd better fly*
if I'm to visit all these heavenly places.

I show the mag to Fox who grins:
Those pretty pics are chosen well
to hollow out your pocket.
Better far to stay at home and find
a hundred ways to fix a tidy profit.
Ignore the hint of what's to come.
'Before you die' is there to scare
the dollars out of ageing pussy-cats.

Angel overhears and growls
Forget Great Walls and Golden Gates!
Don't give Antarctica another thought.
The flights you need to make before you die
require reflection not a boarding pass.
*The hundred things to **do** are all within.*
*Or things to **un**do as the case may be...*

17. He just won't stop

Angel just won't stop. He'll ask
How often do you think of food and sex?
How often do you gripe and curse?
How often do you check your watch?
How often do the dead speak in your dreams?
Do tell me, are you slightly colour-blind?
What do you know of Avogadro's constant?
What's your favourite constellation? Why?

It's been like this for years. He never says
Now just relax and let your neurons idle.
Oh no, it's like – *Let's talk today of the Tao and Analects*
and, if there's time, explore the Second Law
of Thermodynamics. Or I'll hear:
Tomorrow we'll consider semi-colons
together with Krafft-Ebing's work on sexual neurosis.
There may be a connection.

It's every day the same.
He just won't stop.

18. *Lighten up!*

Fox tells me *Come on! Lighten up!*
Forget the body-bags he says.
Forget the skulls.
Forget the refugees all skin and bone.

Don't kid yourself says Fox
there's red-hot-nothing you can do
about all that.
Not you. Not anyone.

So lighten up! Relax! Enjoy yourself!
Go find some well-appointed bar
and sip champagne and laugh!
Sit in the sun!

You won't be always here he grins,
so make the most of what you've got.
Don't twitch and moan and fret about
things you have no purchase on.

Fox riles me. I'm provoked to say
I'd find it abject to ignore
the skeletons and body bags
and refugees all skin and bone.

Your choice says Fox. *It's not a happy one.*

20. Impatient capital

Idly, I ask Fox for his foxy take
on how to make the most of life.
He smirks and tells me *It's a squeeze-*
It's there to flatter, fondle and to seize
for everything it's got.
The goal is High Net Worth and then hole up
for a long and lazy finish, sip by sip.
A villa in the sun. A pool. A yacht.

Angel overhears and snaps: *It's **not**!*
Life lets you open lines of moral credit,
build ethical portfolios
of patient capital, invest
in fixed-return securities.
That's how to make the most of life.
That's what you need to know.

But where I ask him *can one find the Bank*
that handles moral credit?
It's not so much a Bank he smiles,
as holdings in a beneficial Trust
in which all may enrol for life
with rights, if things go well,
to full redemption.

Fox scoffs.
*A coddling Trust! No spine in **that**!*
No challenge, no adrenalin,
no chink of heavy winnings!
All feeble dribbling down the pitch –
no mesmerising shots at goal!
Your 'patient capital' is paralytic!
*You need **impatient** capital to win!*

He/

He makes a call. We hear him say
Put five grand on the favourite.
No, make that eight. No – ten.
Each way.

25. Grievance

Be wise says Angel. *Don't delay*
in mending fences which have failed.
Restore! he urges. *Reconcile!*
Grievance, unattended, scars.
It's like an ulcer which drills down
and suddenly it's gone too far.

Fox disagrees. He hoards offence
however long ago, however small.
He strokes and grooms his grievances
and takes them for long walks on which
he casts around for stones to hurl
as pay-back when the right time comes.

28. Will you fight?

Out of the blue the Angel asks,
Facing injustice will you fight?
Or bow your head and acquiesce,
defer, kow-tow, succumb, submit?

I find that choice too stark and say
I'd need time to assess the threat.
The best course might be wait till dark
and beat a tactical retreat.

Oh no says Angel. *In your dreams!*
It's dark already. Time's run out.
There's not a corner where you can't be seen –
no hole where shirkers can sit tight.

I huff, *Perhaps I'm being slow*
but what in heaven's all the fuss?
Says Angel, *Soon enough you'll know.*
What's coming will be obvious.

Fox listens hard. His ears are sharp
for signs that all may not be well.
This isn't Angel on his usual harp.
His nose detects a pungent smell.

He twitches at the thought of force.
Whatever comes, he'll duck a fight.
Let angels bleed, thinks Fox. *I choose*
to stand well back, play dumb, keep out of sight.

When the smoke has lifted, he'll emerge
from hiding, see who's smiling, and ensure
he lines up smartly with the winning side.
He tells himself he wasn't born to lose.

29. Catching the tide

Never mind the swill says Fox,
the garbage bobbing on the tide,
the sewage floating in the flood.
The key thing is to catch the flow,
to catch the water when it's high.

Angel has no time for tides
and those who try to catch their flow.
He dreads the waste when they recede,
the broken docks, the ruined piers,
the wreckage when the waters go.

30. Vision

Exultant Angel speaks of joy,
exclaiming that *there's nothing like enough.*
I ask what joyfulness he thinks we lack,
and why.

His thoughts are not on pantomime and farce,
on whoop and cackle.
It's joy in ***finding*** that he has in mind –
the sharp delight that comes he says,
when sudden understanding sparks
a quiver of elation and transcendence –
a visionary gleam – a revelation.

I venture *Don't you think that sounds*
a little bare and rarefied?
The clothes of joy are much more sensual –
they flounce and flare!

And also fade, he says
and fall apart, or go
completely out of fashion.
What's well-constructed in the mind
takes hold. It stays.
The rest is nothing more
than passing satisfaction.

Fox/

Fox, tuning in, exclaims
There's nothing wrong
with passing satisfaction!
It's written in the genes!
It's why we're here!
Your momentary intellectual twitch
is no exception.
Like sex, like everything,
it won't last long.

Angel murmurs *That's not so.*
You fail, my friend, to understand
that sensual pleasure's not at all the same
as joy of spirit – the delight that comes
when new paths open for the mind.

New paths for the mind! gibes Fox.
Your visionary sparks aren't going to change
the way **my** *daily world goes round.*

Angel shakes his head. *You're wrong.*
The world's great axis is discovery,
revolving day by day round **how** *and* **why**.
And vision isn't marked 'for angels only'.
It leaves its mark on everyone.

Fox, unregenerate, retorts
It's yet to leave its mark on me!

Contracted out

The Passport Office, long since privatised
and charging what the Government describe as
entirely realistic fees
refers enquiries to Palermo.

What's left of legal aid's contracted out
to a cheerless firm in Kazakhstan
which *never fails*, the Government says,
to give consistent value.

The revenue from captive grids
of all essential services –
the water and the power and the gas –
flows glittering to all parts of the globe.

And your next door neighbour's never seen:
she runs casinos in Hong Kong.
Her house is dark; the only sound
comes from a tripped alarm.

Ode to the higher gardening

for Sarah

Nine boxes punctuate your plot.
In each the earth's composted and raised up
a hand-breadth closer to your hand.

Yes, nine of them there are –
nine prominent no-nonsense shrines
to the muse of cultivation

each with its own hard-hammered plinth,
its timber pedestal; each served
week-in week-out with copious libations.

This is the future. This way you advance,
just slightly bent, to the higher gardening,
to raised-bed mastery;

no longer down on bended knees,
no longer grounded and subservient
to the bindweed that grows deep and never dies.